Kait currently resides in sunny Florida with her family and many pets.

Although she has always been an avid poetry writer, her typical day includes working as a Project Manager for a busy marketing company. Originally from upstate New York, Kait attended Stonehill College in Massachusetts where she studied Communications and Business Administration.

Kait began writing poetry at a young age and soon found it to be a healing way of expressing deep and complex emotions. Recently, Kait has decided to share these expressions with her readers.

To the ones that came on this adventure with me; Mom and Dad, I will never be able to thank you for your unwavering support and unconditional love. Thank you.

Kait Graham

THE HEARTBREAK ADVENTURE

AUSTIN MACAULEY PUBLISHERS™

LONDON • CAMBRIDGE • NEW YORK • SHARJAH

Ordering Information
Quantity sales: Special discounts are available on quantity purchases by corporations, associations, and others. For details, contact the publisher at the address below.

Publisher's Cataloging-in-Publication data
Graham, Kait
The Heartbreak Adventure

ISBN 9781638294832 (Paperback)
ISBN 9781638294849 (Hardback)
ISBN 9781638294856 (ePub e-book)

Library of Congress Control Number: 2022916692

www.austinmacauley.com/us

First Published 2023
Austin Macauley Publishers LLC
40 Wall Street, 33rd Floor, Suite 3302
New York, NY 10005
USA

mail-usa@austinmacauley.com
+1 (646) 5125767

White Mess

Slipping on the white dress
Oblivious to the impending mess

Ready to marry my one and only
Never knowing I would end up lonely

Believing this was the beginning of it all
Believing you would break my fall

But as I tumbled, tear by tear
Waiting for you to stop my fear

I realized then that you weren't there
A truth to admit, I could not bare

Missing

Blue reflection growing dim
Light no longer within

But look close…

A sliver of the old…

A person that once was…

Now silence is the only sound
As she stands and looks around

The Defense Game

Purple
Blue
Because of you

Crushing me with your sobbing sorry
Positioning the heavy shield
Building the barrier to pause your pain

Sweeping away the cruel words
Lifting the rug
Concealing truth in lies

Stepping back
Admiring the impassable walls
All from the outside

Bury

I'll bury you, you said
Except I wasn't dead

Your head hung low
Your eyes were red

I pretended it was all a liquid dream
I pretended I didn't want to scream

Bruised Ego

Examining my pain in the mirror
Realizing life wasn't any clearer

Poking your head in
Tears forming on your lids

Pouring guilt into my throat
Telling me it wasn't you that made me choke

Forbidden

The sticky bar under my arm
My hazy head tired with pain

Strange eyes meeting mine
Searching for anything I could find

Your hand against my cheek
A touch of warmth and deceit

You asked if I was alone
And if I wanted to go home

The reply was yes, let's say goodbye
And the truth is, that wasn't a lie

Tangled

Smooth flesh meeting mine
A finger running through my hair
A touch so unfamiliar, I almost couldn't bare
Gasping with guilt
A heart deeply deprived
Trying not to cry in joy
Hard stares and tears of passion
And then a formal goodbye

Guilty Exchanges

I pull up on the dirt road
My heart already beginning to erode

You stare at me, beer in hand
I wave with innocence that even I can't stand

I'm sure you can see the guilt seeping through
But strangely, you smile as if you never knew

Realizing that you will never tell
And I'll just repent in my own special hell

You

A glass of wine poured
A night alone ahead
And then I check for you

Staring at a strange reflection
Water gliding through tired hands
A glimpse to the side

Suddenly shaking with shock
Watching wine stain the sink
As I call to share

Met with drunk static
A distant drop of my heart
A lonely joy setting in

But I rub you gently,
Smile easing a pained face
Realizing I'm not alone at all

Burn

The light in your eyes
Dim and glossy
The familiar slur of your words
The sting of your tongue
Dipped in Jameson and hate
Frustration boiling below
Burning my lungs
Tearing at my chest
But I keep quiet
Words are only wasted breath

Blind

In front of me, you dress
Baring your real, angry soul
Before cloaking it in cotton

Shielding my eyes
Suppressing my mind
Pretending it was you all along

Promises

Holding his sweet head
Kissing his baby lips
I promise him the world

The feeling of guilt
Creeping in
Promises I can't even keep for myself

Hold On

Daggers stabbing at my heart
Muted pain rising to pursed lips
Threatening the practiced smile
Weak eyes holding fierce to the last tears
Refusing to spill my pain
For I know, I will have to mop the floor

The Blacksmith

Pulling down your mask
Shielding yourself from the jagged shards

I lie waiting
Chisel in hand

Positioned over the heart
The chipping begins

Flinching
One piece at a time

Disintegrating into dangerous dust
Stinging the atmosphere

Staring down at your creation
A beautiful, black abyss

Run

I hear the truck come in with a roar
I go to greet you at the door

Met with eyes, wild and red
Wondering if it was something I said?

I follow asking, what is wrong?
Wondering why you've been gone so long?

I question the smell seeping through your skin
Asking you calmly to let me in

Your hand tight around my arm
As I brace for the impending harm

Crashing into the bathroom sink
Not even knowing what to think

As I back up, I begin to pray
Hoping that this isn't the day

Spewing venom about my death
I close my eyes and hold my breath

I knew then that this was done
I knew then that it was time to run

Disconnected

You call
I snap

I speak more gently
You speak more harshly

Wires are crossed
Sparks ignite

And there is a click
Silence

The Ring

Tight on my finger
Suffocating my heart

Reflecting in the yellow, lamp light
Pulling it away from my skin

Staring at the white engraving
A reminder of a love lost

Pulling out the drawer
A tear sneaking by

Putting it down
Locking it away

A dark, unfamiliar space
Never to see the light of day

The Light

Your sobs soak me through the phone
Telling me you're lost and all alone

But where were you when I lost my way?
Where were you to make everything okay?

And now you force me to carry this guilt
Holding my heart hostage with these walls you've built

But I keep on chipping away
Knowing there will be a better day

Searching for a glimpse of a distant light
Trying not to lose this fight

Refusing to stay locked in this game
Because all the lies still sound the same

Under the Surface

Keeping despair tucked below the soul
Refusing to let it surface
Refusing to let it take hold

Slipping
Lurking
Under these masks

Despair
Waiting to attack
Raw and angry

Waiting to unleash
Wails of fire
That would never cease

But until then,
Despair
Must wait

Goodbye

I see your face on the phone
And I know you're there all alone

I see your eyes following mine
Looking for a hopeful sign

But I refuse to look
Knowing all the courage it took

To put me before you
And everything I had to do

But it doesn't mean I don't want to reach out
It doesn't mean I don't want to cry and shout

And I say I love you too
And remember when we said I do

But I can't bring myself back
Because I know all the things you lack

As I gain strength everyday
I know I must just walk away

I Wish

Staring in my baby boy's eyes
Not yet knowing that life is full of lies

I wonder how I will one day tell him
Dreading a look of blame or sadness

Something I can't kiss away
And then, I wish you weren't here at all

Who Are You?

The boy with the long, blond hair
The one without a care

The one who so gently held my hand
The one that picked my wedding band

But you gave it all away
Pulling back your heart, and all you had to say

Who are you? I would yell
Feeling trapped in this frustrating hell

Refusing to embrace this life
Refusing to work through the strife

The day you left without even a goodbye
Who are you, I wondered as I laid down to cry

The Bad Nights

A lonely flutter of doubt dancing to the surface
Missing you

Missing laughter
Missing touch

Missing jokes
Missing your kiss

But so much has been broken
Repair is impossible

And I must dredge on
Deeper into the unknown

Lonely

These moments
Quiet moments
Wind whispering
Sun retreating
Baby sleeping

These moments
Are the darkest
With my blanket of loneliness
Covering
Tightening

Forcing out a sigh
Holding
Bracing
But don't dare cry
That flood will drown us all

Red

Red ash swirling over glass
Dripping with pain and fear
Shame and guilt bubble to the surface
As I drink the last drop
Splashing me with anger
And watching me drown
Then you walk away without a sound

Heartbreak

Melting my head into the couch
Body succumbing to the floor
Tears staining my fake, brave face
Letting a muffled sob escape

I want to scream
I want to wail
I want to throw things
But the baby is sleeping

Picking up my heavy head
Eyes wet and worn
Pushing up my body
Tired and weak from this journey

And I go on…

The Calm

The tide rolls in
The sun begins to set

The calm washing over me
I feel the end

Rolling tears and wet dunes
Coming to a halt

Night air encompassing me
Warm salt water spray

As I whisper to myself,
"You're almost there…"

Never Ending

Feeling your hand on the small of my back
Taking everything inside me not to retract

The hints of hope that line your smile
The comments about "it just taking a while…"

But I'm sorry to say, it's come to an end
Nothing will fix this, and I won't bend

So please just let me be alone
Please don't continue to cry on the phone

Please just let me be free
Please just let me take care of me

But your selfish ways are never ending
Never letting my heart do any mending

Always there to sweep my good day away
Always there to say what you need to say

So I continue to wait
Until the day you realize your fate

Sign Here

Ink seeping through the pages
Eyes full of fear
Legal jargon mixed with love
Wondering how we actually got here

No More

Do you have any love left for me?
And he knows the answer
But he doesn't know the journey

It's relentless on the soul
It demolishes the spirit
It destroys the heart

So please, no more questions

My soul is empty
My spirit is gone
My heart is broken

Haunted

Haunted by anger
Haunted by you

Dreams descend
Nightmares steal possession

Threatening the air
Suffocating the silence

Feeling the evil pressure
Hovering over my heart

Thankful

Wrapping your arms around my neck
Letting out a joyful giggle
Yelling "Mama" as you squeal
Kissing my lips
Recharging my soul
Mending my heart
And suddenly, I feel alive

The Build

Shaking hands
Brick by brick

Fumbling cautiously
Through rubble

An infant fortress
Standing alone

Until you return
To tear it down

Debris everywhere
Exposing weakness

As I begin again
To build the wall

The New Era

Ping of the phone
Desperation jumping

Fumbling hands
Weak mind

I beg you
Please handle with care

The Date

Stomach flickering with hope
Hiding the brightness
Fear rushing in
So fragile, yet ready
Re-opening my soul
Gentle steps
The glue on my heart still drying
One hard breath
Could shatter it all

Untangle

Feeling veiled anger
Biting words you want to say

Moving boxes
Untangling lives

A crash
A kick

Broken shells
Under my feet

Anxious breaths
Cautious words

Pausing new life
To finish the old

Pier

Damp, night air
Sea swirls below
Hands discovering waist
Mouths entangled
Body awakening
Passion swells
Slamming the pier
I want to hold this
I want to keep this
I want this

Healing

Bright stars pepper the night sky
A fresh breath fills empty lungs

A distant chirp
Trees sway and rustle with warmth

How have I been missing all of this?
Mother Nature gently taps me on the shoulder

Whispers a breeze
"It's OK, you're back now…"

The Meeting

As you pulled out the chair
You met my gaze with such a stare

Ocean blue eyes capturing me
A feeling I couldn't comprehend

Wondering if you could see my concealed soul
As I tried to hide the road I've been on

But as you took my hand so gently
I realized that you could see,
Even the parts I didn't like of me…

Our Love

Sails in the windy night
Whispers of love sliding through
Waves breaking
Hands shaking
Finding a love so true

Pouring pain into the bay
Promising to forever stay
Sipping spirits
Dancing dizzy
Fears vanishing away

Moonlight rhythms
Breaths of relief
Soul sharing
Heart baring
And it all begins with you

Layers

Peeling back the dark
One layer at a time
Even I didn't know what you would find
But you held me close
You said it was OK
Tender hands holding mine
Soaking you with roaring tears
Spilling raw anger
I tried to make you leave
But you refused
Pulling back another layer

Backlash

Your crazy soul taking my heart by storm
The moment we met, I knew you weren't the norm

Carefully removing the Band-Aids from my heart
Giving me a safe place to heal and start

Slowly, I let my head get away
Telling you my stories, and all I had to say

I wanted you more than you will ever know
But you broke me again when you said you had to go

Sometimes I wonder how much this soul can take
Sometimes I wonder when I will break

And finally I realized I never will
All this pain has already led to the kill

The Real

The real was going to come without a doubt
But I wish it wasn't with such an angry spout

I wanted to be the perfect one
The one who laughs, loves and has all the fun

But it was only a matter of time before the real
Only a matter of time that I could conceal

The one I truly am
That one who doesn't really give a damn

The one that's a lost and lonely soul
The one who longs, but has no control

But once the real comes through
There will no longer be a me and you

And how good it was when it lasted
How I wish so bad that I could have masked it...

I See You

You put on your gloves to tend to my heart
I began to believe this would be a fresh start

But as my hurt began to show through
I started to see a new, malicious you

Using shards from my own soul
To manipulate and take control

But I see what you are trying to take
I see through all the fake

I see you for who you are
As I collect another scar

Trust

The truth
Your heart
A slow reveal…
Did I get it wrong again?
Shoving away love to protect myself
Pretending you were someone else
How can I trust?
If I can't even trust myself…

Crush

Just a shell

I look around

Is that my heart on the ground?

It wouldn't be the first time you stepped on it

As I take it back and bite my lip

Snakes

Past and future collisions
Clouding bleary visions

Head swirling all around
Body falling to the ground

Tired of belligerent lies
Tired of crying eyes

Shedding the dead skin of everyone
Time for this to all be done

Open Wound

Shaking hands
Desperately gripping
Trying so hard this time
Trying to make you mine

Bare wounds still open
Fresh stitches holding together
Trying so hard this time
But you can't be mine

Selfish

Past trauma bangs on my chest
Sharp memories pierce my mind
Tired muscles bare my burdens
As you try to help carry it all…

But I slowly pushed away
How dare you try to heal my pain?
This is all of mine to keep
I'll never share, for I'm not weak

Pause

Deep breaths
Steady hands
Thankful thoughts

Epiphanies of love
Realizing it's OK to need
And pause…

Slow breaths
Warm hands
Open mind

Come back my love
Realizing it's OK to share
And pause…

My Baby Boy

Holding your hand
Kissing your cheek
Head resting on mine

Spreading infectious wonder
Exploring with chaotic curiosity
Laughing with innocent joy

Your love lifts me
Your love creates light
Even on the darkest days

Hearts intertwined
You are my one true love
And how great a love story it is

Growth

Planted in the driest ground
Forced to grow without being found

Holding tight to each drop of rain
Using it to feel true pain

Slowly roots began to spread
Refusing to be left for dead

Carefully twisting all around
Refusing to stay so tightly bound

One day, that small sprig broke through
And was greeted by a warm, yellow hue

The Next Chapter

Finally ready for it all,
To live life without fear of a fall

Maybe I won't be "fixed" today,
But that doesn't mean I'm not OK

Feeling a grateful force come over me
Leaving the past where it needs to be

Welcoming self-love with open eyes
No longer hiding behind old lies

Letting each day slowly unfold
Letting go of the story I've told